a collection of delicious recipes

jams
chutneys, pickles, preserves

Contents

Text by James Phillips.

This edition published in 2009 by L&K Designs.
© L&K Designs 2009
PRINTED IN CHINA

Publishers Disclaimer

The recipes contained in this book are passed on in good faith but the publisher cannot be held responsible for any adverse results. Please be aware that certain recipes may contain nuts.

Introduction

When it comes to jams, chutneys, pickles and preserves, you may not know what the difference is between them, but this book holds all the answers! Preserves have been made for thousands of years, and although they were most popular in the days before fridges and freezers, many people still enjoy making homemade jams and other such condiments.

It may seem easier to buy your preserves in your local supermarket, but it's surprisingly easy to create your own in the comfort of your own home. And the cost is far lower, especially if you grow your own fruit and vegetables, and there's always the additional benefit of a greater resulting taste too!

In this book you will find hints and tips on how to perfect the art of making jams, chutneys, pickles and preserves, and with simple step-by-step recipes, it couldn't be easier! One of the most important things a beginner can learn is to make sure all your equipment is sterilized and squeaky clean! Bacteria has a devastating effect on your finished product, so ensure everything is clean and ready to use before starting.

Pectin is also a vital ingredient in the jam-making process. For anyone in the unknown, pectin is the gelling agent to harden your jam, and turn it from a sweet juice into a jelly-like consistency. Pectin is rich in some fruits, which are listed in this book, but for those fruits which lack in pectin, it is available in most supermarkets in a liquid or powdered form.

Chutneys and pickles do not require pectin, and are different to jams as the fruits and vegetables are preserved in vinegar. The acetic content of the vinegar should be 5% or more, and this information can be found on the bottles. Malt or white wine vinegar are the best vinegars to use.

Marmalade is similar to making jam, in that it needs pectin to set correctly, but usually citrus fruits are used. In England, Seville Oranges are the most popular fruit to use (thus called, as they were originally imported from Seville in Spain) but other fruits such as limes and grapefruits also work well.

It is worth noting that most preserves, especially jams, contain a lot of calories, so should be used sparingly by those on weight-control diets. One tablespoon of jam will contain around 70 calories, which may not seem like much, but once you start indulging yourself in your delicious homemade jam, it can be hard to stop!

So, if you want to become a master of making conserves, then make sure you kit yourself up with the necessary equipment. If you are to become a seasoned pro, then it is worth investing in high-quality equipment with a long life span. It may cost that little bit extra, but in the long run, it is definitely worth it!

Definitions and equipment

Jam

Making jam uses fruits and sugar. Sugar has a hardening effect, so when using soft skinned fruits (strawberries etc.) then the fruits should be soaked in the sugar first. This will keep them hard, and help to keep the fruit whole in the finished jam. On the contrary, hard skinned fruits should be simmered before adding sugar to the pan. Fruits which are high in pectin (the substance used as the gelling agent) are best for making jam, because using fruits lacking in pectin will mean your jam will not set properly.

To extract pectin from fruits, they must be softened thoroughly. As a result, when the sugar is added, the boiling process enables the pectin and sugar to mix, causing your jam to set properly. Fruits high in pectin also contain more acid which helps with the pectin extraction. Here is a quick guide to show which fruits are high in pectin, and which are low in pectin.

Fruits rich in pectin
Blackcurrants
Cranberries
Redcurrants
Plums
Gooseberries
Cooking Apples
Damsons
Quince

Fruits medium pectin
Fresh Apricots
Loganberries
Raspberries
Blackberries (Early)

Fruits low in pectin
Cherries
Elderberries
Pears
Blackberries (Late)
Strawberries
Rhubarb

For fruits that lack in pectin, there are 3 ways in which you can make up the deficiency:

- Mixing a low or medium level pectin fruit with a high one e.g blackberry and apple jam.
- Adding lemon juice or citric acid.
- Adding commercially made pectin, which comes in either liquid form or a powdered form.

When using commercially made pectin, ensure you follow the instructions per the packet. A general guide is about 75ml of liquid, or 4 tablespoons of powder, to every 450g of fruit. If you use lemon juice, 3 tablespoons to every 2kg of fruit is sufficient. To test for pectin, take 1 teaspoonful of juice from the pan, place it into a glass, and then add 3 teaspoonfuls of methylated spirit.

If a large clot forms, then pectin is readily available in the juice, and you will get a good set. If the clot is thready and small, then add some more lemon juice/packeted pectin, and continue simmering until you obtain a good clot.

If you want to test for a set, then place 4 saucers into your fridge just before you start cooking the fruit. When you have boiled the jam for the given amount of time, remove the pan from the heat and place a teaspoonful of jam onto one of the chilled saucers. Allow it to cool in the fridge for approximately 5 minutes, then push it with your finger. If a crinkly skin has formed, then your jam has set. If not, continue to boil for another 5 minutes, then test it again (repeat until the crinkly skin forms).

An alternative way of testing for a set (usually the most accurate) is to dip a sugar thermometer into a bowl of hot water, stir the jam and then place the thermometer into it. Ensure that the thermometer does NOT touch the bottom of the pan, as it will likely break. If the temperature is around 105C/220F, then you have reached the setting point.

And the third way in which you can test the setting point is to dip a wooden spoon into the jam, remove it, and after 5 seconds, tilt it so the jam drops onto a plate. If the drops run together in large flakes, then you have reached your setting point.

One of the most important rules about making jam is to ensure your pans, spoons and jam jars are thoroughly cleaned and sterilized, as bad bacteria will ruin your jam.

Pickles

Making pickle is similar to making chutney by the simple fact that they are both preserved in vinegar and assorted spices. However, that is where the similarity ends. Pickles do not need to be cooked for as long as chutneys, with the exception of fruit pickles, where the fruit is heated gently to allow the fruit to absorb the spices and the vinegar. And as chutneys use a variety of fruits and vegetables, pickles are usually based around one.

A quick note when making pickles is to use stainless steel pans, rather than iron or brass pans, as the vinegar reacts with these and will give the pickle a metallic taste (this also applies when making chutney).

Stainless steel pans are cheap and available from all good homestores and supermarkets.

Vegetables used for pickling are first soaked in brine (salt and water solution) for up to 48 hours. This procedure removes the excess moisture in the vegetables, aiding them to stay crisp, and preventing the development of bad bacteria. After the salting process, the vegetables must then be rinsed clean in cold water and well drained before being packed into jars and coated in vinegar.

If you want to use brine, the general mixing recipe is 100g coarse salt to every 1 litre of water. However, if you want to use the dry salt method, then layer the vegetables and salt, finishing with a layer of salt. For every 450g of vegetables, use a tablespoon of salt. If possible, try and avoid using table salt as this will make the pickle cloudy. Coarse salt, sea salt and cooking salt produce better results. Fruits used in making pickles tend to be the larger ones - pears, apples and peaches. Berries tend to go mushy and can be very unpleasant to eat. With fruits that are picked whole, such as cherries and plums, they should be pricked before the preliminary cooking, otherwise they will shrivel up and dry out. Larger vegetables such as cucumbers, cabbage and marrows are best if they are cut into small pieces, but smaller vegetables like onions (the smaller pickling variety) and mushrooms, can be left whole, and will only require peeling. Tomatoes should be halved, and the pips removed.

Relish

Relish is a very versatile preserve, and can be used with lots of dishes. Cold meats, salads and cheeses are great to enjoy relish with, and they can also be added to stews, casseroles or as accompaniments to curries. Relishes use vinegar, like chutney and pickles, although the finished texture is a lot different to those of chutneys or pickles. Not all relishes require cooking, so the ingredients keep their shape. It also means they're quicker to make than any of the other preserves!

Chutney

Chutneys are made from chopped fruits and/or vegetables which are mixed with spices, vinegar and other ingredients, and then reduced to a smooth pulp. The success of making a good chutney is for it to be smooth in texture and have a rich, mellow flavour. To achieve this, it requires long, slow cooking and then, ideally, it should be left to mature for 3-6 months.

A quick tip when using hard fruits such as apples and onions is to soften them in a small amount of water in a covered pan. After this however, the remainder of the cooking should be done in an open pan, as evaporation of the liquid is a vital part of the cooking process of chutney.

When choosing which vinegar to use when making chutney, always look to check it has an acetic content of 5% or more. Malt or white wine vinegar are recommended. You should always aim to use brown or granulated sugar when making a chutney, as it gives a darker colour to the chutney, which is often preferred. If you do want a lighter coloured chutney, then add the sugar only after the fruit and/or vegetables are already soft and mushy.

Generally, whole spices are used rather than ground ones, with the latter creating a muddy, murky effect on the chutney. Bruise these, and tie them in a muslin bag with the other spices.

Marmalade

Marmalade making is very similar to jam making, but the rind needs much longer cooking time, so more water is needed generally. The fruit is simmered until the rind is soft, and the volume of liquid has reduced by about half. Jelly marmalades are made in the same way, but are strained through a jelly bag, and then strips of rind are added.

Any citrus fruit can be used when making marmalade, such as lemons, bitter or sweet oranges, tangerines, nectarines, grapefruits and satsumas. These fruits work best because there is a lot of pectin in the pith and peel of citrus fruits, which is why this is used in the cooking process. Extra acid is often used however to create a good set, as only about 450g of fruit is needed to make 1.5kg of marmalade.

Flavourings such as whisky, rum, brandy and treacle can be added for an added twist, however the citrus fruit must be the main ingredient in your marmalade.

Making marmalade uses the same equipment as jam making, but you will need a juice extractor - more so for making marmalade than jam - but these are cheap as chips in supermarkets!

Equipment

When making a jam, chutney, pickle or preserve, there are a couple of key items which you will need to ensure your jam making experiences run nice and smoothly!

Wax Circles

Immediately after the jars have been filled (remember to leave about 1/2-inch headspace!), wipe the rim clean and place a wax circle on before putting the lid on. The circle should be absolutely flat on the jar to prevent mould.

Jars

Any type or size of glass jars may be used for storing your jam, providing you have cleaned and sterilized them thoroughly. Jars should be heated before putting your jam into them, as putting hot jam into a cold jar may cause it to crack. To sterilize a clean jam jar just before filling, put into an oven at 140C/275F/Gas Mark 1 for 3-4 minutes. Alternatively, you can microwave your jars to sterilize them - fill the jar with cold water, seal the lid and give it a good shake. Remove the lid before putting it into the microwave. Set the microwave to full power and microwave for 1 minute. Everywhere that the moisture has touched around the jar will be sterilized so ensure you wash the water all around the jar. Once the minute has elapsed, empty the water, and your jar is now sterilized.

Plastic screw-on lids are ideal for the top of jars, or cellophane wrapping tied together by string. Try to avoid using rubber bands as these can perish during storage.

Labels

Pretty and decorative labels are of course optional, but give a fantastic edge to your jams, rather than plain old boring white labels. Decorative labels for jam jars are available in all supermarkets, and stationery outlets. It is worth noting the date on which you made your jam/chutney etc, so you know how long it has been maturing in the cupboard!

Preserving pan

When making small quantities of jam, you can use heavy-based saucepans or pressure cookers. But if you want to become a seasoned jam-maker, then it is definitely worth investing in a preserving pan. They can be quite expensive, but good quality pans have a life-span of 20-25 years!

Sugar thermometer

These can be very useful to test that the setting point has been reached, and is generally the most accurate, but it is worth placing your preserve on a saucer and checking the wrinkly-ness! Make a quick note to yourself to never use a sugar thermometer in the microwave as it will crack.

Wooden spoon

It is also worth investing in a long-handled wooden spoon to mix your jam with, as well as a reliable set of scales and a heatproof jug.

Basic Microwave Method

Most preserves and conserves can be made in the microwave. Here is the general method for making jam.

A large microwave bowl, two or three times as large as the volume of jam, should be used and it is important to remember that when you add the sugar to the boiled fruit, the bulk will double.

1. Cook the fruit on full power for around 4 minutes until it is soft. Stir in the sugar until it has dissolved and then cook again on high power for 3 minutes, before stirring thoroughly.

2. Continue to do this until the jam has cooked for about 18 minutes, or until the jam sets when a little is placed on a chilled saucer.

3. Stir in a small knob of butter or a few drops of glycerine to get rid of any scum. Leave to stand for 5 minutes and then pour into hot sterilized jars and seal.

Safety Precautions

It may seem obvious, but safety in the kitchen is vital when cooking! Here are a few quick tips to remember to avoid any disasters!

- Never let anything boil over - it may burn surfaces, or if it lands on your hand, it will severely scald you (it may be worth putting on some rubber gloves if you think you may get hot liquid on your hands)

- When using a hob, keep flammable objects out of the way of flames (tea towels, muslin bags etc).

- Always remember to never let your sugar thermometer touch the bottom of the pan - it will crack, and you may get glass in your jam!

- Always make sure that berries you may use are edible - you don't want to end up with food poisoning!

Remember everything in this section, and you will be a master jam maker in no time!

Jams

Cranberry Jam

2 cups/200g fresh cranberries
1/2 cup/80g finely chopped red onion
1 1/2 cup/350ml apple cider
1/4 cup/60ml balsamic vinegar
3 tbsps honey
1 tbsp frozen orange juice concentrate
1/2 tsp ground cinnamon
Sprinkle of ground cardamom
Sprinkle of salt
Freshly ground pepper to taste

1. In a medium saucepan over medium heat, add the cranberries, onion and cider, and bring to a boil. Reduce the heat and simmer until the cranberries are soft, for about 5 minutes.

2. Transfer the mixture to a food processor and process until smooth. Scrape the mixture back into the saucepan.

3. Stir in the balsamic vinegar, honey, orange juice concentrate, cinnamon, cardamom, salt and pepper. Simmer until the mixture is thickened, for about 20 minutes. Test for a set.

Cool and store tightly covered in the refrigerator for 3-4 weeks.

Blackberry & Apple Jam
9 cups/1.3kg fresh blackberries
4 cups/450g sliced apples
3/4 cup/150ml water
10 cups/2kg granulated sugar

1. Make sure the apples are finely sliced, and put into a pan with a little bit of water (enough to stop them burning).

2. Simmer gently until the apples are soft. Meanwhile, wash the blackberries, draining them well, and put into a pan with water.

3. Stew until tender, and add to the cooked apples. Add the sugar, and stir well until all the sugar has dissolved.

4. Bring to the boil, and boil rapidly for 15 minutes, or until the jam sets when tested. Remove the scum, and pot and seal the jam jars.

Green Tomato Jam
24 green tomatoes
7 1/2 cups/1.5kg granulated sugar
4 cooking apples
1 tbsp root ginger
Juice of 2 lemons

1. Wash the tomatoes, then chop them into quarters. Peel and core the cooking apples, and chop into chunks.

2. Put the tomatoes and apples into a pan, and coat with the lemon juice. Bruise the ginger, and tie in a muslin bag and place in the pan. Cover with enough water to come to the level of the fruit.

3. Bring to the boil, and cook until the fruit is tender. Add the sugar, and stir well until it has all dissolved. Simmer, stirring occasionally until of a thick consistency.

4. Remove the ginger and dispose. Pour into sterilized warm jars and cover.

Pear-Apple Jam

6 peeled, cored and finely chopped pears
4 peeled, cored and finely chopped apples
6½ cups/1.25 kg granulated sugar
1/2 tsp ground cinnamon
1/3 cup/80ml bottled lemon juice
1 packet liquid pectin

1. Crush apples and pears in a large saucepan and stir in the cinnamon. Thoroughly mix sugar and lemon juice with fruits and bring to a boil over high heat, stirring constantly.

2. Immediately stir in pectin. Bring to a full rolling boil and boil hard for 1 minute, stirring constantly. Remove from heat, quickly skim off foam and put into sterile jars, leaving 1/2-inch headspace.

3. Wipe jar rims and process for 5 minutes in boiling water bath.

Microwavable Strawberry Jam

500g strawberries (if you want to make blueberry, blackberry jam, just replace the berries with whichever you want!)
1/4 cup/60ml lemon juice
2 cups/400g granulated sugar

1. Place a small saucer in the freezer. Wash the berries and place in a large microwavable bowl. Add the lemon juice and stir well.

2. Microwave on high for 5 minutes until fruit softens slightly. Stir in the sugar and microwave on high for an extra 20 minutes, stirring at 5 minute intervals.

3. Drop a small amount onto the cold saucer and check for the setting point (this may be slightly thinner than usual).

4. Add 5 more minutes on a high heat if needed. When the jam has set, leave to cool for 10 minutes, then spoon into hot, sterilized jars.

Elderflower & Gooseberry Jam

11 cups/2.7kg gooseberries
13 1/2 cups/2.7kg sugar
5 cups/1.1 litre water
12-15 elderflower heads
1 tbsp butter

1. Use slightly under ripe gooseberries and remove the tops and tails. Cut off the elderflower heads stems close to the flowers. Tie the flowers in a piece of muslin bag.

2. Place all of the fruit into a heavy bottomed saucepan and cover with water. Bring to the boil and add the elderflower heads.

3. Simmer, stirring occasionally for 30 minutes or until the fruit is tender. Remove from the heat and take out the elderflower, squeeze then discard.

4. Pulp the fruit, then add the sugar and stir until fully dissolved. Add the butter, bring to the boil and boil rapidly, stirring frequently, for about 10 minutes.

5. Test for a set, and when the setting point is reached, remove from the heat. Skim the surface with a slotted spoon. Pot the jam into sterilised jars.

Carrot Jam

16 fresh carrots
8 cups/1.8 litres water
2 lemons
Granulated sugar
Brandy (optional)

1. Peel and grate the carrots and put them into a saucepan with the water. Bring to the boil and simmer until soft.

2. Put through a blender until pureed. Add the rind and juice of 2 lemons.

3. Return the puree to the pan and heat, stirring constantly, until all of the sugar has dissolved.

4. Bring to the boil and boil for 25-30 minutes, stirring occasionally to ensure the pulp thickens, and the setting point is reached.

5. Remove from the heat and stir in 1 tablespoon of brandy for each 450g of jam (optional).

6. Ladle into hot, sterilized jars and cover immediately. Label when cooled completely.

Caramel Apple Jam
12 peeled and diced Granny Smith apples
1/2 cup/110 ml water
1 tsp butter
1 packet powdered pectin
3 cups/600g granulated sugar
2 cups/400g packed brown sugar
1/2 tsp ground cinnamon
1/2 tsp ground nutmeg

1. Mix apples, water and butter. Cook over low heat, stirring, until apples are soft (but not mushy). Stir in the pectin, and bring to a full boil, stirring constantly.

2. Add sugars, cinnamon and nutmeg. Return to rolling boil and continue to boil, stirring constantly for 1 minute. Remove from the heat and skim the foam.

3. Pour into hot jars, leaving 1/2-inch headspace. Process in boiling water bath for 10 minutes.

Cherry Jam

12 cups/2kg pitted maraschino cherries
10 cups/2kg granulated sugar
2 tbsps red food colouring
1 tsp almond flavouring
Juice of 1 lemon
2 tbsps salt
1/2 cup/115ml water

1. Mix cherries with salt and allow to stand overnight.

2. The next day, wash 3 times and drain. Add water, sugar, colouring, and cook for 5 minutes. Allow to set for 3 hours.

3. Boil for 5 minutes and allow to set for a further 4 hours. When that time has elapsed, boil for 5 minutes, add lemon juice and almond. Seal in jars and refrigerate for 3-4 weeks.

Alternative Cherry Jam

10 1/2 cups/1.8kg cherries
5 1/2 cups/1.1kg granulated sugar
Juice of 2 lemons

1. Wash the cherries and dispose of the stones. Place into a large pan with the lemon juice and simmer gently until the fruit is soft.

2. Add the sugar, and stir until it has all dissolved. Bring to the boil and boil rapidly for 10 minutes, or until the jam sets when tested.

3. Remove the scum, then put the jam into jars, and seal immediately.

Best if used after 2-3 weeks of storing.

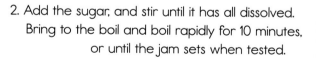

Gooseberry Jam

12 cups/2.7kg gooseberries, slightly under-ripe
13 1/2 cups/2.7kg granulated sugar
5 cups/1.1 litre water
1 tbsp butter

1. Use slightly under ripe gooseberries and remove the tops and tails. Place all of the fruit into a heavy bottomed saucepan and cover with water.

2. Bring to the boil and cook, stirring occasionally for 30-35 minutes or until the fruit is tender. Remove from the heat and pulp or mash the fruit.

3. Add the sugar, stir until fully dissolved. Add the butter, bring to the boil and boil rapidly, stirring frequently, for about 10 minutes.

4. Test for a set, and when the setting point is reached, remove from the heat. Skim the surface with a slotted spoon, and pot the jam into warm sterilized jars.

Cranberry & Orange Jam

4 cups fresh or frozen cranberries
3 cups/650ml water
3/4 cup/175ml orange juice
1/4 cup/60ml lemon juice
4 cups/800g granulated sugar
2 packets/400g liquid pectin

1. Place cranberries and water in a heavy-bottomed pan. Bring to boil over high heat, then reduce heat and simmer, uncovered, until berries begin to pop (about 10 minutes). Drain well, reserving all the liquid.

2. Place cranberries in a food processor and whirl until smooth; add enough of reserved liquid to berries to make 4 cups. Return berry puree to pan.

3. Stir in orange juice, lemon juice and sugar until well blended. Bring to full rolling boil over high heat, stirring constantly, and then boil hard for 1 minute.

Cranberry & Orange Jam/Cont.

4. Remove from heat and stir in pectin at all once. Skim off any foam. Ladle hot jam into hot, sterilized jars, leaving 1/2-inch headspace.

Blueberry-Peach Jam

2 cups/300g blueberries
6 fresh peaches, peeled and chopped
1/2 tsp grated lemon peel
1/2 tsp grated lime peel
Sprinkle of fresh nutmeg
1/3 cup/70g granulated sugar
1 tsp grated citrus peel
1 packet unflavored pectin
1 cup/220ml water

1. In a medium saucepan, combine the fruits and sugar, mashing fruit slightly. Cook slowly for 5 minutes, then boil rapidly for 3 minutes, stirring constantly.

2. Stir in grated peel, and sprinkle pectin over water and leave to stand for 2 minutes. Add to fruit and simmer over low heat for 5 minutes until pectin is dissolved.

3. Cool to room temperature. Pot and seal in warm sterilized jars, and refrigerate for 2 weeks to obtain best flavour.

Strawberry Jam

Approx. 30 fresh strawberries, hulled
4 cups/800g white sugar
1/4 cup/60ml lemon juice

1. In a wide bowl, crush strawberries in batches until you have 4 cups of mashed berry. In a heavy bottomed saucepan, mix together the strawberries, sugar, and lemon juice. Stir over low heat until the sugar dissolves.

2. Increase heat to high, and bring the mixture to a full rolling boil. Boil, stirring often, until the mixture reaches 220F/105C.

3. Transfer to hot sterile jars, leaving 1/2-inch headspace, and seal. Refrigerate for 1 week for best flavour.

Blueberry Jam
4 cups/600g fresh blueberries
2 tbsps lemon juice
4 cups/800g granulated sugar
1 packet fruit pectin

1. Crush ripe blueberries, one layer at a time. Measure into a large saucepan and add lemon juice. Measure the sugar, and set aside.

2. Mix fruit pectin into the blueberries in the pan. Place over high heat and stir until mixture comes to full boil. Cook gently for 1 minute.

3. Immediately add measured sugar and stir. Bring to full, rolling boil and boil for 1 minute, stirring constantly.

4. Remove from heat, skim off foam with metal spoon and ladle into hot jars with 1/2-inch headspace.

(Note: For a more tangy blueberry jam, add 1/4 teaspoon each of cinnamon, cloves and allspice to fruit along with lemon juice)

Apple & Ginger Jam

2 cups/300g fresh ginger roots
8 apples
2 1/4 cups/500ml water
5 cups/1 kg granulated sugar
1 tsp ginger powder

1. Clean the fresh ginger roots and apples and process them in the food processor.

2. Place processed ginger and apples in a saucepan, pour water over them and cook on a medium heat to boil for about 1 hour or until the ginger softens.

3. Place the sugar in the saucepan and cook it for half an hour extra, stirring regularly. Next, stir ginger powder into the ginger apple jam and remove it from the heat.

Pour warm jam into clean jars and seal.

Pineapple Jam

3 cans pineapple chunks
6 cups/1.2 kg granulated sugar
1 tsp citric acid
2 tsps lemon juice
1 tsp pineapple essence

1. Cook the pineapple chunks with water on a low flame. Stir it continuously with a wooden spoon. While it boils slowly add sugar into it. Boil it well by stirring continuously.

2. Test for a set. When the jam is done, add citric acid, lemon juice and pineapple essence to it. Remove from heat and pour into jars.

3. When the jam cools completely, seal the jars. Store in a cool, dark place for 1-2 weeks.

Raspberry Jam

4 cups/800g granulated sugar
4 cups/950g raspberries

1. Place sugar in an ovenproof shallow pan and warm in the oven (250F/120C/Gas mark 1/2) for 15 minutes.

2. Place berries in a large stainless steel saucepan. Bring to a full boil over high heat, mashing berries with a potato masher as they heat. Boil hard for 1 minute, stirring constantly.

3. Add warm sugar, return to a boil, and boil until the mixture will form a gel for about 5 minutes.

4. Ladle into sterilized jars. When completely cooled, seal and store in a cool, dark place.

Mulled Wine & Plum Jam

7 cups/1.8 kg red plums, halved and stoned
Half a bottle of red wine
Mulled wine spices eg. cinammon, nutmeg and cloves
Piece of orange zest without pith
9 cups/1.8 kg granulated sugar
Knob of butter

1. Put the plums and wine into a preserving pan, and place the spices and zest into the pan. Cook gently until the plum skins are soft.

2. Add the sugar, stirring until dissolved. Bring to the boil and boil rapidly for 10 minutes or until the setting point has reached.

3. Add a knob of butter and stir in. Pot into cool, sterilised jars, seal and label when cooled.

Jams

Loganberry Jam

8 cups/1.8 kg loganberries
9 cups/1.8 kg granulated sugar
A knob of butter
Handful of raspberries
Handful of blackberries

1. Prepare the jars by sterilizing them thoroughly. Ensure all of your other equipment has also been cleaned and sterilized.

2. Place the loganberries, strawberries and loganberries in a large saucepan and heat gently, allowing the fruit to cook in its own juices until very tender, about 20 minutes, stirring from time to time.

3. Stir in the sugar and continue to stir until it has dissolved then add the butter. Raise the heat and bring to the boil then continue to boil for about 20 minutes.

4. Remove the pan from the heat and test for a set. If a set has not been reached, contintue for 3 minutes and test again. Continue until you reach a set.

5. Remove from the heat and allow to cool for 15 minutes, skimming any scum from the surface, then ladle into warm jars, cover, seal and label.

Pickles

Pickled Eggs

12-16 hard-boiled free-range eggs
1/2 cup/100ml spiced vinegar

1. Hard boil the eggs, and cool slightly in cold water. (Note: If you stir the eggs gently whilst boiling, it helps keep the yolks in the centre of the eggs).

2. Remove the shells, and pack into clean, sterilized jars. Pour hot spiced vinegar into the jars, then cover and store when cold.

Pickled Onions

6 1/2 cups/1.4 kg pickling onions
1 1/2 cups/450g salt
6 cups/1.4 litres water
1 1/2 cups/400ml spiced vinegar

1. Make a brine by boiling the water and salt together in a pan until all the salt has dissolved. Leave until lukewarm before using.

2. Peel the onions, and soak in the brine for 24 hours, using a plate to keep the onions below the surface of the brine.

3. Rinse the onions well, then pack into sterilized jars, before pouring cold spiced vinegar over them. Cover and label.

For best results and flavouring, leave to mature for up to 6 weeks, in a cool and dry environment.

Pickles

Red Cabbage & Onion Pickle

1 large red cabbage
1 cup/225g pickling onions
1/4 cup/80g salt
1 pint/570ml red wine vinegar
1/4 cup/50g sugar
6 black peppercorns
1/2 tsp allspice
1 medium piece of root ginger
4 cloves
1 cinnamon stick

1. Cut the cabbage into quarters, and wash well. Cut away and dispose of the tough inner core, then shred the cabbage into small pieces.

2. Peel the onions, leaving them whole. Layer the cabbage and onions in a bowl with the salt. Leave to one side for 24 hours.

3. After that time has elapsed, rinse thoroughly in cold water and drain well. Pack into hot, sterilized jars.

4. Put the vinegar and sugar into a small pan. Chop the root ginger, crumble the cinnamon stick, and then put into a small muslin bag with the other 2 spices.

5. Tie the muslin bag up and add to the pan. Bring to the boil and simmer for 15 minutes. Pour the boiling vinegar over the cabbage and onions. Cover and seal the jars. Label jars when cooled completely.

Green Bean Pickle

4 cups/900g runner beans, sliced
4 1/2 cups/900g brown sugar
650g onions, peeled and chopped
3 cups/660ml malt vinegar
1 tbsp cornflour
1 tsp salt
1 tsp turmeric
1 tsp mustard powder

1. Cook the sliced beans in salted water until just soft, and then drain. Cook the chopped onions (don't chop them too finely) in 1 cup of vinegar until soft and transparent.

2. Place the beans, onions and sugar in a pan with the rest of the vinegar and boil for 15-20 minutes. Mix the turmeric, salt, mustard and cornflour with a little bit of cold water and add to the pan.

3. Bring to the boil and cook for a further 15 minutes until of a thick consistency, stirring if necessary to prevent scorching.

4. Pot into hot, sterilized jars but do not seal and lid until completely cooled.

Spiced Pickled Eggs
16 small, free range eggs
1 litre white wine vinegar
2 tsps chopped root ginger
2 tsps allspice
2 tsps black peppercorns
1 tsp salt

1. Roughly crush the black peppercorns and allspice. Place in a muslin bag with the root ginger.

2. Pour the vinegar into a stainless steel saucepan, add the salt followed by the bag of spices.

3. Bring to the boil on the hob, and cover. Lower the heat and simmer for 20-25 minutes. Allow to cool in the pan and leave for 2 hours before removing the bag of spices.

4. Boil the eggs for about 10 minutes. Put into cold water to cool and then remove the shells. Divide the eggs between your jars, and pour the cold, spiced vinegar over them. Ensure the eggs are completely immersed in the vinegar.

5. Seal with airtight lids, and allow 8 weeks before opening again.

Piccalilli

2.7 kg vegetables (Cauliflower sprigs, baby onions, peppers, gherkins etc.)
5 cups/1.2 litres white wine vinegar
1 1/2 cups/450g salt
2 tsps cornflour
3/4 cup/160g granulated sugar
1 tbsp dry mustard
1 tbsp ground ginger
1/2 tbsp turmeric

1. Clean and prepare the vegetables. Spread the vegetables over a large dish and sprinkle with the salt. Place a plate on top of the vegetables and weigh it down, leaving it in a cool place for 24 hours.

2. Drain, wash and rinse the vegetables. Place most of the vinegar, the sugar and spices into a large saucepan, heat gently until the sugar has dissolved.

3. Add the vegetables and simmer gently until the required texture is attained, the vegetables should be crispy and not overcooked. (The level of crispiness depends on personal choice, the vegetables will soften further after pickling).

4. Mix the flour with the remaining vinegar and add to the saucepan. Bring to the boil and simmer gently for 2-3 minutes to cook the flour. Pot and seal.

Leave for 6 - 8 weeks to allow
the flavour to mature.

Pickled Celery

6 Celery stalks
1 tbsp Soy sauce
1 tbsp vinegar
1/2 tsp salt
1/2 tsp granulated sugar
2 drops sesame oil

1. Remove leaves, tough ends and stringy portions of celery stalks, then cut in 1-inch sections. (If stalks are wide, cut lengthwise in half first.) Blanch to soften slightly and place in a bowl.

2. Combine soy sauce, vinegar, salt, sugar and sesame oil. Add to celery and toss well. Refrigerate, covered, only to chill (about 20 minutes).

(Note: If the celery is young and tender, blanching isn't necessary)

Lime Pickle

20 limes, quartered
20 green chillies, tops removed
1/2 cup/150g rock salt
3/4 cup/100g chilli powder
2 tsps ginger slices
1 tsp aniseed
1/2 tsp onion seeds
2 tbsps olive oil
1 tbsp granulated sugar
1 tsp turmeric

1. Put chopped lime pieces into a large pickle or glass jar. Add salt and turmeric. Shake jar to coat all pieces.

2. Add ginger and green chilli to lime. Shake again to mix. Keep aside for 4 days until the lime becomes tender. Heat the olive oil and allow to cool.

3. Crush aniseed, and add all ingredients to the lime pieces. Mix well with a clean dry spoon. Allow 2 days before eating. Preserve in airtight jars.

Pickled Black-eyed Peas

4 cups/1 kg cooked black-eyed peas, drained
1/2 cup/110ml canola oil
1/2 cup/110ml peanut oil
1/2 cup/110ml red wine vinegar
1 clove garlic (leave uncrushed)
1/4 cup/70g red onions, thinly sliced
1/2 tsp salt
Sprinkle of cayenne pepper

1. While peas (either freshly cooked or canned) are draining, create the dressing. Mix the oils, vinegar, garlic, onions, salt and cayenne pepper in a bowl, mixing well.

2. Toss with peas and cover tightly. Refrigerate overnight and remove the garlic. Refrigerate for several days to enrich flavour before serving.

Pickled Cauliflowers

4 cups/900ml white wine vinegar
2 tbsps mustard seed
1 cup/200g granulated sugar
8 whole cloves
4 sticks cinnamon
4 cauliflower heads

1. Simmer all ingredients except cauliflower together for 15 minutes. Meanwhile, wash cauliflower, cutting away all leaves and break into uniform florets.

2. Blanch by putting them into a kettle of boiling water, turn off heat and let stand for 2 minutes. Drain and put florets into jars. Fill jars with strained hot syrup and seal.

Best served after 2-3 weeks of refrigerating.

Pickled Shrimps

12 frozen shrimps in shells
1/4 cup/75g celery leaves
2 tbsps mixed pickling spices
1 1/2 tsps salt
1/4 cup sliced onion
4 bay leaves
3/4 cup/180g low fat Italian salad dressing
1/3 cup white vinegar
1 tbsp capers in liquid
2 drops bottled hot pepper sauce

1. Cover shrimps with boiling water, and then add celery leaves, pickling spices, and salt. Cover and simmer for about 5 minutes.

2. Drain, peel and devein shrimps under cold water. Mix shrimps, onion and bay leaves, and arrange in a shallow dish.

3. Combine remaining ingredients and mix well. Pour over shrimp mixture. Cover and marinate in refrigerator for at least 24 hours, spooning marinade over shrimp occasionally. Pot and seal, and refrigerate for best flavouring.

Pear Pickle

8 cups/1.6kg granulated sugar
4 cups/900ml white wine vinegar
2 cups/450ml water
8 cinnamon sticks
2 tbsps whole cloves
2 tbsps whole allspice
24 pickling pears

1. Combine the sugar, vinegar, water and cinnamon sticks. Add cloves of garlic and allspice tied in a muslin bag. Bring your mixture to a boil and simmer the mixture, covered for about 30 minutes.

2. Wash the pears, remove their skins, and all of the blossom ends. If the pears are large, halve or quarter them for ease of use.

Pear Pickle/Cont.

3. Add drained pears to the hot syrup, bring this mixture to a boil, then lower heat and continue simmering for another 20 to 25 minutes.

4. Pack the hot pears into hot pint jars, and add one 2-inch piece of cinnamon per jar. Cover pears with the boiling syrup, leaving 1/2-inch headspace and making sure pears are completely covered by the syrup.

5. Pot the jars while still hot. Allow to cool before sealing with lid.

Pickled Cucumbers

2 large cucumbers
2 cups/450g salt
Spiced vinegar

1. Wash the cucumbers and wipe clean. Do not peel unless they are bitter. Cut into slices or dice into cubes, and layer with salt in a basin, finishing with a layer of salt.

2. Leave for 24 hours. Rinse thoroughly in cold water and drain well. Pack into clean, sterilized jars and cover with cold spiced vinegar.

Cover and label with contents and date.

Chutneys

3. Place the pan over a high heat and bring to the boil. Reduce the heat to low, and cover and simmer for 45 minutes. (The lemons should be soft at this point. If not, continue until they are).

4. Remove the pan from the heat, and pour the chutney into hot, sterilized jars and seal immediately.

Pumpkin Chutney
1 pumpkin (weighing approximately 1kg) - peeled and chopped
2 cloves garlic, chopped
3 cups/500g tomatoes, peeled and chopped
450ml/2 cups white wine vinegar
1 tsp allspice
1 tsp white peppercorns
3 1/4 cup/650g brown sugar
2 1/4 cups/500g onion, peeled and sliced
1 tbsp salt
1 tsp ground ginger
1 tsp black peppercorns

1. Place the chopped pumpkin in a pan and coat with vinegar. Add the sliced onions, chopped tomatoes and garlic.

2. Crush the allspice and peppercorns, and then add both to the pan. Stir well, and put to one side for 1 hour.

3. Add the ginger and salt to the mixture, then bring to the boil slowly. Simmer for approximately 40 minutes, stirring occasionally.

4. Allow the chutney to cool, then pour into hot, sterilized jars. Cover and seal the jars, and label them when completely cooled.

Best used after 6-8 weeks of maturing in storage.

Chutneys

Hot Aubergine Chutney (Warning - Very Hot!)

1 kg aubergines
3/4 cup/175g soft brown sugar
2 1/4 cups/500g onions
1 1/2 cups/350ml white wine vinegar
1 tbsp tomato puree
1 tsp cayenne pepper
3 tbsps salt
6 tbsps seedless raisins
5 cloves of garlic
3 red chillies

1. Slice the aubergines, put into a colander and sprinkle with salt. Leave for 3-4 hours, then rinse and dry.

2. Whilst leaving the aubergines, put the vinegar, tomato puree, sugar and raisins into a bowl, mix well and leave to stand.

3. Finely chop the onions and chillies and mix with the aubergines, followed by the vinegar mixture, in one large pan.

4. Heat gently, stirring until the sugar completely dissolves, and simmer until the chutney thickens. Pour into hot, sterilized jars and seal.

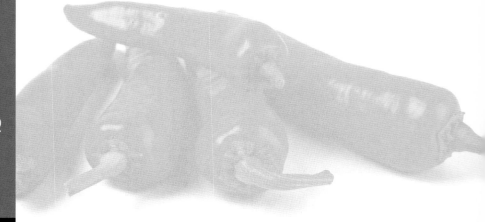

Apple Chutney

8 cooking apples
4 cups/900ml vinegar
1 cup/225g sultanas
1 cup/225g onions
4 tbsps mixed pickling spice
2 tsps ground ginger
1 tbsp salt

1. Peel, core and slice the apples, and then peel and chop the onion. Put them into a pan with the vinegar, raisins and salt. Tie the pickling spice in a muslin bag and add to the pan. Stew the mixture until tender. Remove the spice bag and add the ginger.

2. Add the sugar, and stir well until it has all dissolved. Bring to the boil and boil until the chutney is thick. Pot into hot, sterilized jars immediately and seal.

Apple & Cucumber Chutney

3 cucumbers
8 cooking apples
3 cups/650g onions
2 1/2 cups/600ml white wine vinegar
2 1/2 cups/500g brown sugar
1 tsp cayenne pepper
1 tsp salt

1. Peel, core and chop the apples. Peel and finely chop the onions. Cut the cucumbers in half lengthways, and scoop out the seeds. Chop finely.

2. Place the apples, onions and cucumber into a pan with the vinegar and bring to the boil. Simmer until softened. Add the sugar, cayenne pepper and salt. Stir until all of the sugar has dissolved.

3. Continue simmering until the chutney thickens, stirring occasionally. Pour into hot, sterilized jars and seal. Store for 4-6 weeks for best flavour and taste.

Mango Chutney

2 cups/400g granulated sugar
1 cup/225ml white wine vinegar
6 mangoes, peeled and chopped
1 medium-sized onion, chopped
1 garlic clove, minced
1/2 cup/75g golden raisins
2 tsps finely chopped ginger
1 tsp mustard seeds, whole
Sprinkle of red chilli flakes

1. Combine the sugar and vinegar in a large pot. Bring to the boil, and stir constantly until the sugar dissolves.

2. Add the remaining ingredients and simmer uncovered, until the chutney becomes slightly thickened. Stir occasionally during cooking.

3. Pour into hot, sterilized jars, leaving a little headspace. Seal jars, and allow to cool in a cold water bath for 10-15 minutes.

Beetroot Chutney

8 cups/1.3kg beetroot
1 large onion
1 cooking apple
2 cups/400g granulated sugar
2 1/4 cups/500ml white wine vinegar
2 tsps root ginger
1 tsp salt

1. Cook the beetroot, and dice into small 1-inch pieces. Peel and dice the onion and apple.

2. Place the beetroot, apple and onion into a large pan with the sugar, ginger and vinegar.

3. Bring to the boil and simmer until the ingredients are soft. When they have reached an optimum softness, ladle into jars and seal.

Red Tomato Chutney

6 lbs/2.7kg red tomatoes
4 large onions
1 3/4 cups/350g granulated sugar
1 1/3 cup/300ml malt vinegar
2 tbsps salt
2 tsps paprika
1/2 tsp cayenne pepper

1. Wash and chop the tomatoes, then peel and chop the onions. Place the tomatoes and onions into a heavy bottomed saucepan, cook gently to release the tomato juices, and simmer for approximately 20 - 30 minutes until tender.

2. Add the salt, paprika, cayenne and half of the vinegar, cook gently for 45 minutes or until it begins to thicken. Add the sugar and remaining vinegar, stirring until fully dissolved.

3. Continue simmering, until the mixture becomes thick, stirring occasionally. Leave for 3 - 5 weeks to allow the flavour to mature.

Date & Orange Chutney

4 medium oranges
3 1/4 cups/750g granulated sugar
7 tbsps golden syrup
2 tbsps coarse salt
1/4 tsp crushed dried chillies
6 3/4 cups/1.4 litres malt vinegar
2 1/4 cups/500g onions, chopped
500g dates, stoned and chopped
Handful of raisins

1. Grate the orange zest and set aside. Remove the pith from the oranges and discard the seeds. Finely chop the orange flesh.

2. In a large, stainless steel saucepan, combine the sugar, syrup, salt, chillies, and vinegar. Bring to a boil over high heat, stirring to dissolve the sugar.

3. Add the oranges, onions, dates, raisins, and half the grated zest.

4. Reduce the heat and simmer until thick, for about 1 hour. Stir in the remaining orange zest.

5. Spoon into warm, sterilized jars. Leave to cool, then seal. Store in a cool, dark place.

Apricot & Date Chutney

12 dried apricots
2 large handfuls pitted dates, chopped
3 cups/600g brown sugar, firmly packed
3 cups/450g golden raisins
2 cups/450ml white wine vinegar
2 cups/450ml water
1 tbsp mustard seed
1 tbsp salt
2 tsps ground ginger
1 tsp ground coriander
1/2 tsp ground nutmeg

1. Soak the apricots in enough water to cover for 30 minutes. Drain and put into a large saucepan. Add the dates, brown sugar, raisins, vinegar, water, mustard seed, salt, ginger, coriander, and nutmeg.

2. Simmer on low heat until thickened, stirring frequently to prevent sticking, 45 minutes to 1 hour.

3. Ladle hot chutney into sterilized 1/2-pint jars, leaving 1/2-inch of headroom.

4. Run a rubber spatula around the insides of the jars to release trapped air bubbles.

5. Wipe the rims of the jars with a clean cloth. Place lids in position and tighten the screwbands.

Chutneys

Kiwi Chutney

14 kiwis, peeled and sliced
2 bananas, peeled and chopped
3 sweet onions, chopped fine
Grated zest of 1 lemon
Juice of 3 lemons
1 cup/140g raisins
1 cup/200g brown sugar, packed
1 tsp ground ginger
1/2 tsp cayenne pepper
1/2 tsp ground allspice
1/2 tsp freshly ground nutmeg
Sprinkle of ground cardamom
1 tbsp sea salt
1 cup/220ml white vinegar

1. Place kiwis, bananas, sweet onions, lemon zest, lemon juice, raisins, brown sugar, ginger, cayenne pepper, allspice, nutmeg, cardamom, salt, and white vinegar into a heavy saucepan.

2. Bring to a boil, lower heat, and simmer uncovered for approximately 1 hour until thickened.

3. Pour into dry, sterilized jars, and allow to cool before sealing.

Blackberry Chutney

1 tbsp olive oil
1 red onion, finely chopped
Handful of ginger, finely chopped
2 large red chillies, finely chopped
2 1/4 cups/500g blackberries
3 tbsps caster sugar
2 tsps red wine vinegar

1. Heat the olive oil in a large saucepan. Add in the red onion, ginger and chilli. Fry gently for 4-5 minutes until softened. Add blackberries and cook for 3-4 minutes, stirring occasionally. Add in the sugar and vinegar, mixing well.

2. Bring to a boil and simmer for 15-20 minutes until thickened. Allow to cool before spooning into hot, sterilised jars. Cover with waxed paper discs and cool. Once cooled, seal and store until using.

Plum Chutney

3 cups/500g dark red plums
2 shallots, chopped
1 tbsp olive oil
1/2 cup/110ml white wine vinegar
3 tbsps water
1 cinnamon stick
1/2 cup/100g demerara sugar

1. Cut the plums in half down the crease, twist the halves in opposite directions and pull apart. Prise out the stones and discard. Roughly chop the flesh. Place the chopped shallots in a stainless steel saucepan with the olive oil and heat until sizzling. Sauté gently for 5 minutes until softened.

2. Add the chopped plums, vinegar, water, cinnamon and sugar. Stir until the sugar has dissolved, then simmer for about 15 minutes, stirring occasionally, until softened and slightly thickened. Meanwhile, heat the oven to 120C/250F/Gas Mark 2. Place a clean medium-sized jam jar in the oven to warm. When the plum chutney is ready, spoon it into the warm jar. Seal with a lid and leave to cool completely.

Apricot, Apple & Peach Chutney

2 sour cooking apples, peeled, cored and coarsely chopped
1 can dried peaches
4 dried apricots
1/4 cup/50g sultanas

6 garlic cloves, peeled and mashed to a pulp
2 cubes ginger root, peeled and finely grated
2 cups/450ml white wine vinegar
2 cups/400g caster sugar
2 tsps salt
1/2 tsp cayenne pepper

1. Combine all the ingredients in a heavy stainless steel pan and bring to the boil.

Turn heat to medium-low and cook, keeping up a fairly vigorous simmer, for about 30 minutes or until you have a thick, jam-like consistency.

2. Stir frequently and turn the heat down slightly when the chutney thickens as it could stick to the bottom of the pan.

3. Let the chutney cool. It will thicken some more as it cools. Pour into a clean jar and cover with a non-metallic lid.

Store in a cool place or keep in the refrigerator.

Apple & Cranberry Chutney

10 cooking apples, peeled and chopped into small chunks
4 eating apples, peeled and chopped into large chunks
6 large onions, sliced
2 tbsps fresh root ginger, finely chopped
1 tsp peppercorns
2 1/2 cups/500g granulated sugar
1 cup/230ml cider vinegar
2 1/2 cups/500g cranberries

1. Place all ingredients except cranberries in a large stainless steel saucepan, then gently heat, stirring, until the sugar dissolves.

2. Bring to the boil, then reduce heat and simmer, uncovered, for about 50 minutes, stirring regularly until the apples and onions are tender, the mixture has thickened and no watery juice remains.

3. Add the cranberries, then cook for a further 10 minutes or so until just softened but not burst.

4. Spoon the hot chutney into sterilised jars and seal. Store unopened in a cool, dark place. The chutney will keep for up to 6 months.

Chill on opening.

Chutneys

Hot Peach Chutney (Warning - spicy!)

12-16 sliced peeled peaches
1 cup/165g raisins
2 cloves garlic, minced
1 large chopped onion
3/4 cup/140g chopped preserved ginger
1 tsp chilli powder
1 tsp mustard seed
1 tsp pickling spice
Sprinkle of curry powder
4 1/2 cups/900g packed brown sugar
4 1/4 cups/950 ml apple cider vinegar

1. In a large heavy pot, stir together the peaches, raisins, garlic, onion, preserved ginger, chilli powder, mustard seed, curry powder, brown sugar and cider vinegar. Wrap the pickling spice in a muslin bag, and place in the pot.

2. Bring to a boil, and cook over medium heat uncovered until the mixture reaches your desired consistency. It will take about 1 1/2 hours to get a good thick sauce.

3. Stir frequently to prevent scorching on the bottom.

4. Remove the spice bag, and ladle into hot sterilized jars. Wipe the rims with a clean moist cloth. Seal with lids and rings.

Lime Chutney

12 limes, halved (24 halves)
1 medium onion, peeled, quartered
4 hot green chilli peppers
1 inch ginger root
6 cups/1 kg seedless raisins
7 green cardamom pods
1 tbsp black peppercorns
1 tbsp coriander seeds
1 tbsp mustard seeds
4 dried red chilli peppers
1 1/2 cups/350ml cider vinegar
3 tbsps coarse salt
2 1/4 cups/450g light brown sugar.

1. Juice the limes. Discard 6 lime halves. In a food processor, combine remaining 18 lime halves, green chilli peppers, ginger and raisins. Chop finely. Place mixture in a non-metal bowl.

2. Open the cardamom pods. In a heavy skillet, toast peppercorns, cardamom seeds, mustard seeds and coriander seeds and the dried red chillis for about 3 minutes, stirring constantly.

3. Add spices, lime juice, sugar and vinegar to the chopped fruit mixture. Stir thoroughly, cover and allow to marinate at room temperature for two days.

4. On the third day pour mixture into an enamelled pot, add salt and bring to a boil slowly. Simmer, uncovered, for 30 minutes. Fill into prepared clean jars.

5. Close jars with a tight fitting lid. Store in a cool place. The chutney should rest for at least 2 weeks (4 weeks recommended) before opening. Keep open jars in the refrigerator.

Chutneys

Lemon Chutney

8 lemons, cut into 1/4 inch slices
1 cup/220ml wine vinegar
2 medium onions, thinly sliced
1 large garlic clove, thinly sliced
2 tsps cinnamon
6 cloves
2 bay leaves
1/2 tsp chilli powder
3 1/2 cups/700g brown sugar

1. Put lemon slices in a saucepan with water to cover. Bring to a boil. When boiling, reduce heat to low. Simmer, covered for 2 hours. Add water if too much evaporates. When finished there should be 1 cup/220ml of liquid.

2. After measuring, put back in saucepan with other ingredients except sugar. Return to the boil.

3. When boiling, pour in sugar. Cook, stirring until sugar is completely dissolved, then lower heat and cook until thickened and leaves a trace on a wooden spoon, but has not gelled. Pack into sterilized and clean jars.

Relishes
&
Jellies

Tomato & Celery Relish

1 onion
1 large green pepper
1 large celery
2 cans chopped tomatoes
1 tbsp salt
2 tbsps sugar
2 allspice berries
2/3 cup/150ml vinegar

1. Mix all the ingredients in a large bowl. Heat a pan gradually to the boiling point.

2. Add all the ingredients into the pan, and cook slowly for 1-2 hours. Allow to cool before serving, or potting.

(Note: Cayenne pepper or mustard may be added if desiring a more seasoned relish.)

Sweet Onion Relish

9 cups/2.2 kg sweet onions, finely chopped
2 red bell peppers, washed, seeds and stems removed, finely chopped
1/4 cup/65g sea salt
1 cup/200g granulated sugar
1 cup/220g light brown sugar, packed
1/2 tsp ground turmeric
2 cups/450ml cider vinegar
1 tsp mixed pickling spices

1. Combine the chopped onions and bell peppers with the salt. Stir and let stand for 30 minutes. Bring a saucepan of water to a simmer, reduce heat to low and add the jar lids. Keep them in the hot water, but do not boil.

2. Half fill a canning kettle with water, add the jars and bring to a boil. Reduce heat to low and keep jars hot while the onion mixture is simmering.

3. Drain the vegetables in a sieve, squeezing gently. In a large stainless steel pot, combine the sugars, turmeric, and vinegar.

Sweet Onion Relish/Cont.

4. Put pickling spices in a muslin bag and add to the vinegar and sugar mixture. Bring to a simmer, then reduce heat to low and simmer gently for 5 minutes.

5. Add the well drained vegetable mixture, increase heat to medium, and bring to a boil. Lower heat to medium low and simmer for 30 minutes.

6. Fill the hot jars and wipe rims with damp paper towels. Fit the jars with the lids and screw jar rings on firmly.

Tomato Ketchup

2.5kg ripe tomatoes
1/2 cup/100g granulated sugar
2 tbsps dry mustard
1 tbsp ground allspice
2 cups/450ml cider vinegar
3 tbsps salt
1 tbsp black pepper
1 tsp ground cloves

1. Select good, ripe tomatoes. Scald and strain through a coarse sieve to remove seed and skin. Allow to cool.

2. When the tomatoes become cold add the remaining ingredients. Allow to simmer slowly for 3 hours, before pouring into hot jars, and sealing.

Beetroot Relish

4 cups/550g chopped raw beetroots
6 cups/875g chopped cabbage
2 cups/450g chopped onions
2 cups/400g granulated sugar
2 tbsps prepared horseradish
1 tbsp salt
2 cups/450ml vinegar

1. Combine all ingredients in a large pot. Bring to a boil, reduce heat, and simmer for about 20 minutes, or until thickened, stirring occasionally.

2. Pack into hot sterilized jars and process for 20 minutes in a boiling water bath.

Creamy Cucumber Relish

1 long cucumber, grated
2 tbsps sour cream
1 tbsp fresh dill, finely chopped
1 tsp jalapeño, minced
1/2 tsp garlic, minced
Sprinkle of sea salt
Sprinkle of black pepper

1. Seed the cucumber (if not using English cucumber), otherwise, coarsely grate cucumber.

2. Place cucumber into a sieve and squeeze out all the excess moisture. Mix cucumber and remaining relish ingredients together in a medium bowl.

Refrigerate until ready to use.

Apricot Jelly

24 large apricots
12 1/2 cups/2.5 kg sugar
2 lemons
4 tbsps vanilla sugar
4-5 tbsps rum (optional)
2 packets liquid fruit pectin

1. Wash and divide apricots in halves, process them in a food blender and pour into the saucepan together with sugar.

2. Wash the lemons and cut them in slices together with the skin. Add lemon slices in apricots and cook on a low temperature to soften for about 30 minutes. Stir the vanilla sugar, rum and pectin in the apricots, cook it about 3 minutes more and remove it from the heat.

3. Pour hot fruit jelly in the sterilized and warm jelly jars, cool them and seal them when completely cooled.

Pear Jelly

2.2 kilogram cleaned pears
Juice from 1 lemon
Juice from 1 orange
2 packets liquid fruit pectin
12 tbsps sugar
1/2 tsp powdered cinnamon
1/2 tsp powdered cloves

1. Blend the washed and cleaned pears. Pour blended pears, lemon juice and orange juice in the saucepan.

2. Pour the sugar, cinnamon and cloves over fruits in the saucepan and cook the jelly in low heat to boil for about 30 minutes (stirring it all the time).

3. Stir the pectin in the fruits, cook it 5 minutes more and remove it from the heat. Pour hot fruit jelly in warm, sterilized jars, cool them and seal them at the end. Store the pear jelly in a cool and dark place.

Cherry & Almond Jelly

3 1/2 cups/750ml cherry juice
4 1/2 cups/900g granulated sugar
1 packet liquid pectin
1 tsp vanilla extract
1 tsp almond extract

1. Bring 1 cup of cherry juice, vanilla and almond extract to a boil. Boil for 1 minute. Add remaining juice and pectin and return to a boil.

2. Boil for 1 minute. Add sugar and bring to a full rolling boil. Boil for 2 minutes.

3. Pour into clean, sterilized jars and seal when cooled,

Red Wine Jelly

1 1/2 cups/330ml red wine
2 tbsps lemon juice
1/4 cup/55ml orange juice
2 tbsps orange liqueur
3 cups/600g granulated sugar
1 packet liquid pectin

1. Combine wine, juices, and liqueur in top of double boiler. Stir until the sugar is dissolved, for about 3-4 minutes.

2. Remove from heat. At once, stir in liquid pectin and mix well, before skimming off foam. Pour into sterile jars leaving headspace.

3. Wipe jar rims, adjust lids and rings. Fill and seal each remaining jar.

Corn Relish

8 fresh corn on the cobs
8 chopped green bell peppers
4 chopped onions
1 coarsely chopped unpeeled cucumber
4 cups/750g chopped red ripe tomatoes
4 cups/900ml vinegar
2 cups/400g granulated sugar
1/4 cup salt
1 tbsp turmeric
1 tbsp mustard seed

1. Remove corn from the cobs and combine prepared vegetables in a large pot. Add vinegar, sugar, salt, turmeric, and mustard seed, and mix well.

2. Heat to boiling, and simmer for 25 minutes or until the vegetables are tender. Seal in hot, sterilized canning jars, and lid when completely cool.

Mango Relish

Juice of 1 large lime
3 mangoes, peeled & diced
8 peaches. peeled & diced
1/4 tsp coriander
5 serrano peppers, diced
1/4 tsp ground allspice
4 green onions, finely chopped
1 tbsp fresh mint
2 cloves garlic, finely diced
3 tbsps fresh coriander, chopped
1 tbsp fresh chives, chopped
Salt & pepper (to taste)
3 tbsps tequila (optional)

1. Place the mangoes, peaches, pepper, onions and garlic in a bowl, and cover with the lime juice and tequila. Separately, mix well the rest of the ingredients, and then gently toss into fruit.

2. Adjust salt and pepper to taste, and add more lime juice as needed. Cover, then pot and seal. Refrigerate at least an hour before serving.

Cranberry Relish

1 orange, peeled and quartered
2 cups/350g fresh cranberries
2 apples, unpeeled and diced
2 cans pineapple chunks, drained
3 tbsps granulated sugar

1. Place the orange in a food processor and process until coarsely ground. Spoon into a medium bowl and set aside.

2. Repeat with the cranberries. Combine all ingredients in a medium bowl and mix well. Cover and chill for 8 hours, before potting and sealing.

Rhubarb Jelly

8 crab apples, washed and chopped
4 3/4 cups/900g rhubarb, washed and chopped
5 1/2 cups/1.2 litres water
75g sugar per 100ml liquid

1. Place the apples and rhubarb in a heavy-bottomed saucepan along with the water. Bring to a boil, reduce to a simmer and cook for 30 minutes, until the apples are very soft.

2. Pour into a jelly bag lined with several layers of muslin and allow to drain into a bowl.

3. The following morning discard the fruit then measure the volume of the liquid and add 75g sugar per 100ml of fluid.

4. Place the juice and the sugar in a saucepan, heat through then add the sugar, stirring until completely dissolved. Bring to a boil and cook rapidly for about 15 minutes. Test for a set. Continue until a set has been reached.

5. Skim the surface then ladle into sterilized jars that have been warmed in an oven set to 100C/200F for 5 minutes. Allow 1/2-inch of headspace then secure the lid, allow to cool and store.

Blackberry Jelly

1.8kg blackberries
1 1/3 cup/300ml water
Juice of 2 lemons
1/4 tsp mace
1/4 tsp nutmeg
1/4 tsp cinnamon
375g sugar per 500ml juice

1. Wash the blackberries thoroughly and drain in a colander. Add the fruit to a pan along with the water, spices and lemon juice. Bring to a simmer and stew until the fruit is soft (about 1 hour).

2. Turn into a jelly bag or a colander lined with two layers of muslin or cheesecloth and leave to strain over night.

3. The following day measure the volume of juice and heat in a pan. Add 375g of sugar per 500ml of liquid and stir until all the sugar has dissolved. Bring the syrup to a boil and continue boiling rapidly for 10 minutes.

4. Test for seting at this time. If it's not ready boil for a further five minutes then test again. Remove any scum from the top of the jelly then pour into cleaned and sterilized jars that have been warmed in an oven.

Seal securely and store.

Champagne and White Grape Jelly

1 bottle champagne
2 cups/450ml white grape juice
11 cups/2.2 kg granulated sugar
2 tsps unsalted butter
4 tbsps lime juice
2 packets liquid fruit pectin
1 1/2 cups/350ml red grape juice
Zest of 1 lime

1. Combine 2 cups of champagne, the white grape juice, and 7 cups of sugar in a large saucepan over high heat. Bring to a rolling boil and add 1 tsp butter, 2 tbsps lime juice, and 1 packet of pectin.

2. Boil for exactly 1 minute and remove from heat. Sterilize ten 1/2-pint jars. Ladle the hot mixture into the hot jars so that each jar is half full. Cover until set (6 to 12 hours).

3. Combine remaining champagne, sugar, lime juice, red grape juice, and lime zest in a large saucepan over high heat. Bring to a boil and stir in the remaining butter and pectin and cook for exactly 1 minute.

4. Carefully pour over the top of the champagne jelly, leaving 1/2-inch headspace. Securely cap each jar and store in a cool, dark pantry for up to 1 year.

Redcurrant Jelly

7 cups/1.3 kg fresh redcurrants, stemmed
1 2/3 cup/170g granulated sugar
6 fresh sage leaves

1. Bring the redcurrants and 1 cup of water to a simmer in a covered wide-bottomed pot. Cover and bring to a simmer. Mash the berries and cook over medium-low heat for 10 minutes.

2. Uncover, reduce heat to low, and simmer for 5 more minutes. Rinse a muslin bag with hot water.

Redcurrant Jelly/Cont.

3. Squeeze dry and use to line a colander set over a large bowl. Pour the currant mixture into the colander and let drain for at least 5 hours. Do not press.

4. Place two small saucers in the freezer. Add the sugar and sage to the strained liquid and transfer it to a wide-bottomed pot. Bring it to a boil over medium-high heat, skimming off the foam, until the mixture reaches 220F.

5. Remove from the heat and test the consistency by placing a teaspoonful onto the chilled saucer. If it does not gel, continue to cook a few more minutes and repeat the test. Pick out the sage leaves and pour the jelly into clean jelly jars.

6. Allow to cool, and then store refrigerated jelly for up to 1 month.

Other preserves

Kiwi & Lime Marmalade
4 kiwis, peeled and trimmed
Zest of 1 lime, slivered
3/4 cup/150g granulated sugar
2 tbsps fresh lime juice

1. Cut the kiwi into quarters, and then cube them into 1/2-inch cubes.

2. Combine the kiwis with the remaining ingredients in a casserole dish and stir well.

3. Cook, uncovered in the microwave on a high heat for 5 minutes. Stir well, and return to the microwave, and cook until thick, for another 6 minutes.

4. Allow the marmalade to cool to room temperature, then cover tightly and refrigerate for up to 2 weeks.

Tangerine Marmalade
18 tangerines
2 lemons
1 grapefruit
28 cups/7 litres of water
450g of sugar per pint of juice extracted

1. Wash and dry the tangerines, lemons and grapefruit. Cut them in half, and squeeze out the juice, before removing the pith, pips and inside skin.

2. Cut the peel finely, then tie the grapefruit peel, lemon peel, pips, inside skin and pith in a piece of muslin.

3. Put the tangerine peel in a large bowl with the muslin bag of peel and pics etc. Add the squeezed juice, 7 litres of water and mix well. Allow to soak overnight.

4. Next morning, turn the contents of the bowl into a preserving pan, bring to the boil and simmer gently for 2 hours, removing the muslin bag after 1 hour. Turn the contents of the pan into a jelly bag and leave to strain overnight.

Tangerine Marmalade/Cont,

5. Measure the juice and put into a pan to heat. Add the correct amount of sugar, and stir until the sugar has dissolved.

6. Add shredded tangerine peel, bring to the boil, and then boil rapidly until the marmalade reaches setting point.

7. Remove the scum, and allow to cool for 15 minutes. Pot and seal whilst still warm.

Orange Marmalade

6-8 small oranges
Juice of 1 lemon
6 1/2 cups/1.4 litres water
5 1/2 cups/1.1kg granulated sugar

1. Slice the oranges in half. Using a metal spoon, scoop out the flesh over a bowl to collect any juice, leaving the pith behind. Reserve the shells. Put the flesh, juice and pips in a food processor and blend until smooth.

2. Push the purée through a sieve into a preserving pan. Scoop out as much of the pith from the shells as possible. Slice the rind into very thin matchstick strips and add these to the sieved flesh in the pan.

3. Pour in the lemon juice and water. Bring to the boil. Reduce the heat and simmer for 1 hour until the rind is soft and the mixture has reduced by half.

4. Over a low heat, add the sugar and stir until it has dissolved. Boil for about 10 minutes, skimming off any froth on the surface. Test for a set, then allow the marmalade to cool slightly, then pour into the sterilized jars.

Strawberry Conserve

8 cups/1.8kg strawberries
9 cups/1.8kg granulated sugar

1. Wash and hull the strawberries, drying thoroughly. Place the strawberries in a large bowl with alternate layers of sugar, then cover and leave in a cool place for 24 hours.

2. Place the fruit and sugar mixture into a heavy bottomed saucepan, bring to the boil and cook for 5 minutes, stirring occasionally.

3. Return the mixture to the bowl, cover with a cloth and leave for 48 hours. Place the fruit and sugar mixture back into a heavy bottomed saucepan, bring to the boil and cook for 10 - 15 minutes, stirring occasionally.

4. Cook until the setting point is reached, then pot. (N.B This does not set as firmly as most jams.)

Carrot Marmalade
2 cups/450g carrots
2 lemons
1 orange
4 cups/800g granulated sugar
Boiling water

1. Wash and peel the carrots. Squeeze juice out of lemons and remove seeds. Put carrots and lemon rind through food chopper.

2. Cut the orange into very thin slices and remove seeds. Combine all the ingredients and add 1/2 cup/115 ml boiling water. Cook until the mixture gels. Pour marmalade into jars and refrigerate for 2-3 weeks for best flavour.

Grapefruit Marmalade
6 grapefruit
4 lemons
1 cup/220ml cold water for each 75g of fruit
45g sugar to each 50g of fruit/water

1. Cut each fruit in quarters and slice the quarters through pulp and rind as thin as possible, discarding all seeds.

2. Weigh the prepared fruit and add 1 cup/220ml of cold water to each 75g of fruit. Set aside for twenty-four hours.

3. Boil gently until the rind is perfectly tender, then set aside until the next day. Weigh the material and add 45g of sugar to each 50g of mixture.

4. Leave to cook, stirring occasionally to avoid burning. When it thickens, pour it on a cold dish. The mixture will thicken still more on cooling and care must be taken not to cook it too much. Store as jelly.

Peach Marmalade

1/4 cup/55ml lemon juice
1 small orange, washed
12 ripe peaches, peeled and finely chopped
1 packet powdered fruit pectin
5 1/2 cups/1.1 kg granulated white sugar
1/2 tsp ground cinnamon
1/4 tsp ground ginger
1/4 tsp freshly ground nutmeg

1. Cut orange in half crosswise and remove any seeds. Cut each half into 4 quarters, then thin-slice into wedges that are 1/4-inch thick, including rind.

2. Place orange slices, lemon juice, peaches, and fruit pectin into a heavy pot. Bring to a boil over high heat, stirring constantly. Add sugar and return to a fast boil. Continue to boil for 1 minute, stirring constantly.

3. Remove from heat and skim off any foam. Stir in the cinnamon, ginger, and nutmeg. Pour into sterilized dry jars and seal.

Seville Orange Marmalade
6 Seville oranges
Juice of 1 large lemon
2 1/2 cups/600ml water
6 1/2 cups/1.3 kg granulated sugar, warmed

1. Wash the fruit, then cut it in half and squeeze out the juice. Tie the pith and pips in a muslin bag and shred the peel. Soak the peel and the muslin bag in the water overnight.

2. Put the peel, muslin bag and the water in the pressure cooker. Put on the lid and bring to high pressure. Cook for 10 to 15 minutes, according to the thickness of the peel. Reduce pressure at room temperature.

3. The peel must be really tender before the sugar is added. To test, let it cool, then press a piece of peel between thumb and forefinger. When it is cool enough to handle, take out the muslin bag and squeeze the juice from it into the cooker.

4. Next, add the warmed sugar. Stir over gentle heat until the sugar is dissolved, then boil it rapidly in the open cooker until setting point is reached (sugar temperature should be approximately 105C/220F).

5. Skim if necessary and let the marmalade cool until skin starts to form before pouring it into warm, dry jars. Seal when completely cooled.

Microwavable Orange Marmalade

6 oranges
Juice of 1 lemon
2 1/2 cups/500g jam sugar

1. Cut the oranges into quarters, and remove pips. Put pips and lemon shells into a muslin bag and tie up. Finely slice oranges and put in a bowl with the bag, lemon juice and 300ml boiling water. Cover and soak for 1 hour.

2 Add 200ml boiling water. Microwave on High for 20 minutes, stirring after 10, until peel is tender. Add the sugar and stir to dissolve. Microwave on High for 25 minutes until setting point is reached, Stir and ladle into jars. Seal lids when completely cooled.

Microwavable Red Onion Marmalade

8 cups/1 kg red onions, cut in 1/4-inch wedges
3 tablespoons olive oil
1/2 cup/110ml white wine
1/2 cup/110ml red-wine vinegar
1/2 cup/100g granulated sugar
1 tbsp grenadine
1/2 tsp salt
1/2 tsp pepper

1. In a large glass bowl, combine onion wedges with oil. Cook, uncovered, on a high setting for 8 to 10 minutes, stirring occasionally. Drain and discard any liquid.

2. Add wine, vinegars, sugar, grenadine, salt and pepper, and mix well. Cook, uncovered, on a high setting for 15 minutes, stirring every 3 minutes.

3. Spoon into sterilized jars, and seal with lids when completely cooled. Refrigerate for best flavour.

Pear Honey

24 ripe pears
1 cup/180g diced pineapple
Grated rind and juice of one fresh lime
5 cups/1 kg granulated sugar

1. Wash, peel, and core pears, then run through food chopper, using fine blade. Dice the pineapple and combine with pears and lime rind and juice.

2. Add sugar and cook over slow heat, stirring frequently. Cook for 20 minutes and pack into sterilized jars and seal while hot.

Zucchini Marmalade

4 1/4 cups/800g grated zucchini (leave the skin on)
Juice of 2 lemons
1 tsp grated lemon zest
1 can crushed pineapple (drained)
5 cups/1 kg granulated sugar
2 tbsps crystallized ginger (finely minced)

1. Place zucchini in a pot and add lemon juice, lemon rind and pineapple. bring to a boil and simmer for 15 minutes.

2. Continue to stir until it comes to a boil. Stir in sugar and ginger. Bring to a full rolling boil and boil hard for 1 minute.

3. Remove from heat and stir and skim with a metal spoon for 5 minutes. Pack in sterile jars with sterilized new rings and lids. Cool completely and check to make sure all the jars are properly sealed.

White Grape Jelly

2 bunches of white grapes
1 3/4 cups/350g granulated sugar
1 lemon

1. Wash the grapes, remove from the stalks, and cook them to fall apart. Strain it through a fine strainer.

2. Measure the grape juice, add 350g of sugar and 50ml of lemon juice for every litre of grape juice.

3. Cook the grape juice with sugar and lemon, until the sugar melts and mixture becomes thick (about 30 minutes), and stir it occasionally.

4. Remove foam from surface of the grape jelly preserve with a spoon, pour the hot jelly in the clean warm jars and seal when completely cooled.

Pumpkin Syrup

3 pumpkins, diced
20 cups/4 1/2 litres water
2 1/2 cups/500g granulated sugar
8 lemons, squeezed

1. Cook the cleaned and diced pumpkin in 2 1/2 litres/11 cups of water to soften and cool it. Pour the sugar in 2 litres/9 cups of water and cook it to melt.

2. Allow the sugar mixture to cool and then pour squeezed lemon juice in sugar syrup. Process pumpkin in food processor and mix it with lemon sugar syrup.

3. Pour fruit syrup in clean jars or bottles and store them in the refrigerator for 2-3 weeks for best flavour.

Other Preserves

Citrus Marmalade

2 lemons
1 orange
2 1/2 cups/550ml water
Dash of baking soda
1 large grapefruit
1 packet liquid pectin
6 cups/1.2 kg granulated sugar

1. Remove white pith from peel of lemons and orange. Stack strips, Cut into thin slices.. Combine lemon and orange peels, water, and baking soda in a saucepan. Bring to a boil over high heat. Reduce heat to low. Cover and simmer for 20 minutes, stirring occasionally.

2. Meanwhile, peel grapefruit and remove pith. Discard peel and pith. Separate fruit into sections. With fingers, remove pulp from membrane of each section over large saucepan to save juice.

3. Dice fruit sections into same saucepan. Bring to a boil. Cover and simmer for 10 minutes. Measure 5 cups fruit mixture into a large saucepan.

4. Mix pectin into fruit mixture. Bring to a rolling boil over medium-high heat, stirring constantly. Immediately stir in sugar. Bring to a rolling boil and boil for 1 minute, stirring constantly.

5. Ladle hot marmalade mixture into hot jars leaving 1/2-inch space at top. Wipe the rims of the jars, place wax discs on top and then seal.

Orange & Blackberry Marmalade with Chocolate Chips

4 1/2 cups/1 litre mashed blackberries
3 oranges
5 cups/1 kg granulated sugar
1 cup/200g dark chocolate chips
1 packet liquid fruit pectin

1. Wash oranges, grate orange peel and squeeze the juice from them. Pour sugar, orange peel and juice in mashed blackberries and cook it again (stirring it all the time).

2. When fruit mix starts to boil, stir fruit pectin in. Remove foam from the surface of the marmalade with a spoon and stir chocolate chips in it to melt for a few minutes.

3. Remove blackberry orange marmalade from the heat and give it a good stir. Pour into sterilized warm jars, and seal.

Lime Marmalade
12-16 limes
15 cups/3.4 litres water
30g granulated sugar per 20g pulp

1. Wash and dry the limes. Cut into halves and squeeze out the juices, and remove the pips and pith. Tie these in a muslin bag.

2. Cut the peel finely, and put into a large pan with the muslin bag, and then add the juice. Add the water, and leave to soak overnight.

3. Weigh a preserving pan and make a note of it. Put the soaked peel, pips and pith into it with the water and juices.

4. Bring to the boil, and simmer gently until the peel softens and the contents of the pan have been reduced to half their original bulk. This will take around 2 hours.

5. Lift out the bag of pips and pith, squeezing against the side of the pan with a wooden spoon. Re-weigh the pan, and subtract from that weight the weight of the empty pan, to give you the weight of the pulp.

6. Add the correct amount of sugar compared to the pulp (3 parts sugar to 2 parts pulp) and stir until all the sugar has dissolved.

7. Bring to the boil, and boil rapidly until the marmalade sets when tested. Remove the scum, and then pour into sterilized jars whilst still hot.

Red Grapefruit Marmalade
2 ruby red grapefruit
1 lemon
1 1/2 cups/330ml water
Sprinkle of baking soda
5 cups/1 kg granulated sugar
1 tbsp kiwi juice
1 packet liquid fruit pectin

1. Remove peel from grapefruit and lemon by slicing each into 4 quarters, then separate the skin from the fruit pulp. Reserve the peels. Remove any seeds and white pith from the fruit pulp, chop, and set aside.

2. Cut away as much of the white pith as possible from the rinds and discard. Slice rinds very thin and place in a large saucepan with water, kiwi juice and baking soda.

3. Bring to a boil, reduce heat, cover, and simmer for 20 minutes, stirring occasionally. Add reserved fruit to the rinds and simmer for an additional 10 minutes. Remove all but 3 cups of the fruit mixture and add sugar. Stir to combine.

4. Return to a full boil while constantly stirring. Boil hard for 1 minute, then remove from heat and immediately stir in pectin. Stir and skim off any foam for 7 minutes. Ladle marmalade into hot, sterilized jars and seal.

Roasted Aubergine Marmalade

4 medium aubergines, unpeeled, cut into 1/2-inch cubes
4 tbsps minced garlic
4 tbsps minced fresh ginger
1/2 cup/100g brown sugar, packed
1/2 cup/110ml red wine vinegar
2 tbsps chopped tarragon
1 tbsp sesame oil
1 tbsp soy sauce
2 tsps fennel seeds
1 cup/150ml chicken broth

1. Preheat oven to 400F/200C/Gas Mark 6. Place aubergines, garlic, ginger, brown sugar, wine vinegar, tarragon, sesame oil, and soy sauce in a baking pan. Stir to combine.

2. Bake for about 90 minutes until liquid evaporates and aubergines begin to brown and stick to the pan. Remove from oven. Stir in 1/2 cup of the chicken broth, scraping up any browned bits. Return to oven and bake for another 20 minutes.

3. Remove from oven and stir in remaining 1/2 cup chicken broth, again stirring up any browned bits. Return to oven and bake for an additional 15 to 20 minutes until aubergines are thoroughly browned. Let cool until warm, then refrigerate for up to 10 days. Can also be served cold or frozen for up to 1 month.

Quince Marmalade

3 pounds/1.3 kg quince
5 cups/1 litre water
5 lemons cut in half
6 cups/1.2kg sugar

1. Wipe fur from outside skin of quinces with a damp cloth. Quarter and core fruit reserving all cores, seeds etc. Place reserved cores and seeds in a muslin bag, tied at the top with string.

2. Dice quinces with a knife or food processor. Put into a jam pan with water. Thinly slice lemons and add to pan.

3. Simmer until fruit is quite tender, about 45 minutes. Watch carefully so fruit does not boil over. Warm sugar by placing in a steel bowl in a 250F/120C/Gas Mark 1 oven for 5 minutes. Stir in warmed sugar into jam pan with fruit.

4. Boil rapidly until setting point is reached , by which time quince should be a beautiful rich pink colour. Test a little of the marmalade.

5. If set, pour quince marmalade into sterilized jars, and lid. When completely cool, wipe jars and label. Store in a cool place. Will keep for at least 12 months.

Lemon Marmalade

10 large lemons
4 cups/900ml water
4 cups/800g granulated sugar

1. Remove yellow part of peel in strips from lemons. Cut into thin strips. Cut off all the pith from the lemons.

2. In a heavy saucepan, combine lemon peel, sliced fruit, and water. Cover and refrigerate for 3 to 4 hours. Heat lemon mixture to boiling over high heat, stirring frequently.

3. Reduce heat to low; cover and simmer, stirring occasionally, until lemon mixture is very soft, for about 1 hour. Add sugar to lemon mixture and increase heat to medium-high; stir until sugar dissolves.

4. Heat to boiling and reduce heat just so mixture boils gently. Boil uncovered, stirring frequently for 60 minutes. Spoon marmalade into hot jars, leaving 1/2-inch space at top of jars.

5. Wipe jar rims clean. Seal with lids. Cool jars on wire rack. Label jars, and store in cool, dry place.

Cucumber Marmalade

2 cups/350g finely chopped cucumbers
4 cups/800g granulated sugar
1/2 cup/110ml of lime juice
2 tbsps grated lime peel
1 1/2 packets liquid fruit pectin
Blueberry juice (to colour)

1. In a big saucepan, combine cucumbers, sugar, juice and peel. Mix well, and add the coloring. Boil for one minute over high heat, stirring constantly.

2. Remove from stove, and stir in the pectin. Skim off foam, stir and skim for 5-10 minutes to cool a bit. Ladle quickly into jelly glasses and cover, then seal when completely cool.

Banana Marmalade

12-16 ripe bananas
Juice of 2 lemons
Rind of 2 lemons
5 cups/1 kg granulated sugar
1/2 grated orange

1. Peel and slice the bananas into thin, round slices. Cut out any dark spots.

2. Combine all the ingredients in a large pot, and stir to mix well. Cook over a low heat, stirring until the sugar dissolves completely.

3. Cook, stirring frequently to prevent sticking, for 15-20 minutes, or until the mixture is of desired consistency.

4. Pour into warm, sterilized jars and seal when cooled completely.

My Recipes

My Recipe

Ingredients:

Preparation:

My Recipe

Ingredients:

Preparation:

My Recipe

Ingredients:

Preparation:

My Recipe

Ingredients:

Preparation:

My Recipe

Ingredients:

Preparation:

My Recipe

Ingredients:

Preparation:

My Recipe

Ingredients:

Preparation:

My Recipe

Ingredients:

Preparation:

My Recipe

Ingredients:

Preparation:

My Recipe

Ingredients:

Preparation:

My Recipe

Ingredients:

Preparation:

My Recipe

Ingredients:

Preparation:

My Recipe

Ingredients:

Preparation:

My Recipe

Ingredients:

Preparation:

Index and
Conversions

index

Jams

Pickles

Chutneys

Relishes & Jellies

Other Preserves

The recipes contained in this book are passed on in good faith but the publisher cannot be held responsible for any adverse results. Please be aware that certain recipes may contain nuts. The recipes use both metric and imperial measurements, and the reader should not mix metric and imperial measurements. Spoon measurements are level, teaspoons are assumed to be 5ml, tablespoons 15ml. For other measurements, see chart below. Times given are for guidance only, as preparation techniques may vary and can lead to different cooking times.

Spoons to millilitres

1/2 teaspoon	2.5 ml	1 Tablespoon	15 ml
1 teaspoon	5 ml	2 Tablespoons	30 ml
1-1 1/2 teaspoons	7.5 ml	3 Tablespoons	45 ml
2 teaspoons	10 ml	4 Tablespoons	60 ml

Grams to ounces

10g	0.25oz	225g	8oz
15g	0.38oz	250g	9oz
25g	1oz	275g	10oz
50g	2oz	300g	11oz
75g	3oz	350g	12oz
110g	4oz	375g	13oz
150g	5oz	400g	14oz
175g	6oz	425g	15oz
200g	7oz	450g	16oz

Metric to cups

Description			
Flour etc	115g	1 cup	
Clear honey etc	350g	1 cup	
Liquids etc	225ml	1 cup	

Liquid measures

5fl oz	1/4 pint	150 ml	
7.5fl oz		215 ml	
10fl oz	1/2 pint	275 ml	
15fl oz		425 ml	
20fl oz	1 pint	570 ml	
35fl oz		1 litre	

Oven Temperatures

Gas mark	°F	°C
1	275°F	140°C
2	300°F	150°C
3	325°F	170°C
4	350°F	180°C
5	375°F	190°C
6	400°F	200°C
7	425°F	220°C
8	450°F	230°C
9	475°F	240°C